CLAIMING

Every quick feather asserts a just claim:
it bites like a saw into white pine.
-- William Stafford
"Lit Instructor"

Acknowledgments

Many thanks to the editors of the following journals, anthologies and newspapers in which some of these poems have appeared, some in earlier versions: *The Birmingham Poetry Review*; *Black Fly Review*; *Chants*; *Echoes, The Northern Maine Journal of Rural Culture*; *Exit 13*; *Fat Tuesday*; *Green Fuse*; *Gypsy*; *Kennebec: A Portfolio of Maine Writing*; *Lilliput Review*; *Out of the Cradle*; *Potato Eyes*; *Appalachian Voices*; *Puckerbrush Review*; *Spoon River Quarterly*; *The Snail's Pace Review*; *The Starving Poets' Cookbook* (Free Lunch Arts Alliance); *Thema*; *West Wind Review*; *Yankee Magazine* and *Zone 3*. The *Bucksport Free Press*, *The* [Bucksport] *Enterprise*, *The Ellsworth American*, and *The* [Torrington, Connecticut] *Register Citizen*. In addition to publication in journals above, "Tarpaper" and "Bedding I'd Call Beautiful" appeared in Maine's *Chalkdust*, to whom I am grateful. "For the Love of Learning" was a winner in *The Republican Journal*'s 1994 poetry competition.

CONTENTS

HARKING

For ancestors and living kin — my first and best teachers. Especially my mother, whose handmade notebooks with corrugated cardboard and storm window plastic covers taught me about necessity, about the need to write.

WHERE YOU STEP HERE

You road I enter upon and look around,
I believe you are not all that is here,
I believe that much unseen is also here.

-- Walt Whitman
"Song of the Open Road"

IN THEIR DUST

So rich is the soil with the crumbling bones
of our ancestors...it has been difficult of late
to find six feet of earth not preempted by these pioneers.
                    --The Gray Family of Hancock County, 1903

I.

                Claim the dust now do you?

No. I go to my knees to the tribes
in whose dust we are hateful specks.
Not that forgiveness is possible
but bowing to the record showing
some old love, too, between us.

I shall go back to wherever we're from
however far needed to know. I will dance
in your dust wherever we were, walk grounds
and by waters named for you.
And with feet bared that we might touch,
remembering who we are. Rub
your remains to my skin and in that
recognition believe we go on. Touch
your dust to my tongue to receive
what you would have me say.
When I am finished hope to find
I have become you.

II.
Out of the question to bring a best teapot
to steep again on biscuitwood heat
of brook alder, the taste taking her back
to British beginnings. Or fanciful lace
if only a piece to wear for good or show
on a shelf or save in a chest. *Separatist.*
Exile. Prisoner of conscience to this day.
Still I know she thrilled at the wildness
as much as she wept for the missing
humming Old Country songs at work.

13

How I want her to have admired The First Ones
hoping her young would be as earthly wise.
To have persuaded her husband to settle peaceably
and taught their children to honor the tribes.

I see her with frugal habits making her way
down the years to me, gardens staked
against deer and coon, putting by pork in brine
against winters that would test to the core.

She must have lost children to distance
and not knowing and known pain
of a kind gone with time. Must have danced
in delight for good greens and trout
and whatever mountains and meadows
heaved up each spring.

From my grandmother and mother
and stories of theirs I'd say she lived
in and out of the generations as splendid
as a woman could be, making the way easier
for those of us to come
before turning to soil each time. It's not
without applause that I revere
the very dust of this place.

WHETHER YOU STAY OR GO

Courage is required.
Either way keeps faith
honoring your lines.

You held my hand
when your grandfather
passed into us. Not alone

but in company
with those gone before
and to come. Now, son,

we begin to pass again.
On the island where you live
you are from away.

Though your people
have wintered Maine's cost
three centuries and a third

your name
will engender attitudes
and you will be thought foreign.

Be instructed.
Meet mistrust with respect.
We've worked this outback

for potatoes and pulp. Balanced
to that old echo: *Build
that load! Tread that hay!*

Pitched and walked again
in oven mow thousands
of forks to keep the cows

to keep us
to keep the land.
Whether you stay or go know

you earned the choice
as well as the piece coming to you.
It's all we have to leave.

And our songs.
Let the diamonds
your golden father cut

into the field after haying
each August for family ball
be your jewels. Time with us

your account. This legacy yours
to claim or not. When you cross
the narrows at Trenton consider

the considerable crossings
bringing us all here. May our
small stories be your amulet of rue

to throw as your ancestors oceans ago
on terrifying depths against dreaded
dragons Ignorance and Fear.

Through them we pass to you.

OUTBACK BALL

In the fifties we felt the pull
from Turkey Path and Silver Lake,
Jacob Buck Mountain and Charlie Cole way,
across brooks, *yes marm* roads and hills.

We went every night when night
started at the four o'clock whistle
ending the dayshift, and papermakers
made their ways home to the valley.
Across Millvale, newfangled pressure cookers
helped get meals to tables on time. Nothing
on the few t.v. sets in the neighborhood
but snow from the first station upriver
in Bangor. Dishes done, to the field!

To the game!
To chickenwire backstop, hay stubble, mud.
To hand over hand who picks first from men,
women, kids. Everyone gets to play, little ones
to grands. Every night after supper. To play
until dark in pasture park and hike home
under star-seeded sky to the singing of frogs
and friends. When families played ball outback
after supper.

PATENT LEATHER PRAYER OR
MAY ALL THE CHILDREN HAVE MARGARET
POOLER SHOES SOMEDAY AMEN

She must have been in 6th grade
first time she saw patent leather shoes.
They'd probably been in stores in Bangor
but fancy things were handed down
from cousins in Camden or the one
from Enfield who was Miss Maine in 1947.

Mostly, she and her mother and sisters
made clothes from laying mash material
or prints sent away for that never matched
the catalog. One pair sturdy shoes every fall
to be taken off at home to last. She was

enchanted the first time Margaret Pooler
tapped down the aisle in black shiny shoes,
charmed by their sleek look, classy clicking
on the Jewett School's new tile floor. Imagine: dress
shoes everyday! So taken was she

by these slippers with slight wedge heels
she whisper-asked, having seen her size
at recess trying on turns, if she might have them
when they were worn. "Of course,"
was like having them already and allowed her
back to social studies and math.

She didn't forget but was still suprised
the day the shoes were brought to her
in a bag. Held them to her all the way home
on the bus--patent leather shoes!
Cracked where the toes bent, soles thin,
she didn't care. She watched the way
they looked in a mirror propped low
and listened: Heaven!

It never occurred to her
that when her father arrived home tired
and mean from his shift at the mill, he'd be so mad
for what she'd done. Ordered the shoes back
next day. Now she buys patent leather shoes
for kids when she can. Anonymously.

CHOREOGRAPHY

Saw the word the first time when t.v.
came downriver in the 50s. Not in time
so I'd know it on the college entrance exam,
damnitall. Didn't use that word then, either,
thanks to the brimstone brothers preaching in town
come out to the country to save us and eat around,
shaming us kids guilty of rock 'n' noll and ballgames and
skating. Bad boy-girl stuff like that. Soon's I saw credits
for the June Taylor Dancers on the Ed Sullivan Show
knew I'd missed that one. Well how could I know
if I'd never seen a choreographed anything? Bet
those kids from Boston and New York didn't know what
clabber was or the kind of trip that lifts and drops
a rake of hay in just the right place at the end of a windrow
when you rein the horse right. Or windrow for that matter.
Well I got in. And learned a whole lot of new words.
Some grand, glad to have. Some peculiar in a worthless
sort of way, if you know what I mean. But neither
the college nor the church taught me anything about
words more important (*more*, mind you) than what I knew
from the farm. Nor could they overcome it,
come to think of it, though they sure as hell tried.

TOO LONG AT THE FAIR

You been raisin the deuce again?
                                    -- Ruth Moore, *The Weir*

The cattlebarn kids tired from stall work,
grooming and shoveling, claimed
their fair time. They'd done their jobs
followed rules stayed with their cows
so latecomers could see. Wanting it over
wanting to go home Blue Hill's glamour gone
they passed the word. Some kept watch
and signaled. Some made the hole
in the middle of the aisle where fairgoers
strolled sometimes finding our kids as interesting
as the herds. Tired of being on exhibit
they spread the rut with fresh manure
they were tired of whisking away, prize
or no prize, turning it to ripe tea with hoses
handy for keeping their cows shit free show clean.
Glee! Sifting straw and shavings to camouflage
the place they returned to railings
by Holsteins, Guernseys, Jerseys and kin,
playing nothing-was-up, guarding
the spot with pitchforks and pretense
until worthy candidates entered the far end.

It was awful watching them choose and send signs,
the place renewed between acts:
a bare-chested gold-chained fancy-booted dude,
an uptight yuppy supermom. The kids
fairly fell from the bars in hilarity until someone
looked their way seeking to blame, then
all innocence broke loose and victims decided one
by one either to throw a fit or laugh, either way
entertaining until the call came: *Loademup!*

Last night Blue Hill Fair 1970-something.
God it was fun.

21

CHASING CHICKENS

The afternoon Gina left
we had to chase the bantam
back to the henhouse,
timothy and clover
greener than her yard,
mint, woodruff
a sweeter place to be.
Ed urged one way, I another,
persuading, marking the way,
but she scooted between us
and off she went
as if she'd a mind of her own.

The strawberry patch world
waited.

BARN FREE

They feed themselves. That's what they're for.
                                    -- H.H. Price, *Blackberry Season*

Time was: every barn worth its stock had cats.
Generations worth. Wild. Witty.
Hunting hills of hay, stalking flight-
path and hole for stealers-of-grain.
Prowling hedgerow, aldergrove and field
for guts and gristle, returning
with the cows in single-file parade
to *heahboss* for twice-daily drinks
of white warmth. Cautious friends
of Man the Milker.

Time was: children grew. Cows went to auction.
In quiet stalls the cats waited. Called
to the porch they waited. Missing
as much as Man the Milker, they crept
from hedgerow, aldergrove and field
taking gizzards and gravy and storebought
milk in ready-to-run crouch. Once
he watched a first generation domesticated
barnkit stalk, tease, and pounce on a pencil,
and wept.

Time was: barn came down. Matriarch returned
to deliver in remnant lair
of waiting-to-be-burned wood,
the scent the same only slighter:
ripe rottings turning soil. Man the Milker
knew she'd come back to the pile
as long as it was there. To memory
marked only by manure-tea ash
whose branches still showed the slant
of the roof. He knew *he* would.

ROAD HOME

Millvale slush
through March woods past
where Raymond Bridges just died
his farm stand
his last stand
but didn't he try

boys grunting proud robin's egg wreck
back up the hill *Need a push?*
Sure! sends one to the wheel
the other in barn boots (not Bean's)
thclugg-thcluggs alongside

gum-rubber heels dragging pot-hole tar
plaid flannel shirt under camouflage cap
running his serious stuff signaling man-like:
keep commin! keep commin!
ho!

oh boys
aren't you sons of this place
thank you for being on this road proving
sure as sweet water rises in maples another time
another season of do-it-yourselfers know how
to make do get by
passing it on
passing it down

thanks for the lift

COUSIN RICHARD'S DEAD

We're all headed for boxes
it's clear. His: too early, plain.
They put him in it
in his red plaid woolen shirt.
On his pillow, crumpled hat
and that everlasting icon of death:
tri-colored folded flag,
patriot's reward. His tractor
flipped over on him. Crushed
that fiddle playing russet faced
fellow, that Katahdin keeping
gentlewild man. Now he's returning
to soil in banks of bayland
from which he came, to waltz again
in ancestral dust
in which his children's children
and theirs and theirs
will work and play as long
as earth stays for her own old dance.

BAPTISM AT BLUE HILL

Today you toddle in salt water
your baby feet as worthy of this shore
as those of the rich new as you. This ocean yours
as much as theirs. Your curling toes claiming
tracks of beach for balance. Today
the cove is yours to grab by tiny fistfuls.
To hold earth's brink in your hands: to touch
and taste, yours to play. Today
this briny bay christens you *Maine*. Blessing
your little boy parts when you scootch
to smack the sea here under mountain
heath. Here where ancients
arrive by tide for the event and
changed, unchanged, by your wade,
bow out as sacredly as they gathered in,
knowing something not known before.
Knowing you.

BEDDING I'D CALL BEAUTIFUL

Saw a doe go down last night.
Didn't know what she was doing.
Been watching her on the ledge
flipping flies with earflags and tail
'til she turned to trot along the ridge,
then right to the pond pasture
to graze, I thought. Dropped
before she stopped, it seemed,
sliding intentionally into grass,
front first, disappearing into daisies,
beneath buttercups, bug-bothered knees
probably berry-stained pink, timothy
tickling her soft underplaces. No sign
of that big deer above the straw.
Knew she was there though. Saw myself.
Still I'd be surprised to come upon her,
as if she'd taken secret steps through sod.
Only flattened field to prove the place,
matted hay to mark morning.

WHAT THE FIELDS KNOW

Arthur came *onthebus* when it wound
downeast in the 60s more hair
than his dogs Karma and Krishna he brought by
to run in our fields, Alaskan malamutes
muscling into Maine, until they turned
on our sheep who could have died from fright alone.
Now that he's director of the Photographic Arts
Museum in San Diego--California coiffed--we know
Where The Wild Things Are.

Larry strode our highlands and low
practicing his pipes his daily amount. Glorious
for a MacLellan lass to hear. Gone
but for comical memory of the chickens squawking
to high heaven not knowing the meaning
of their fear only their fear. Outbackers
still talking, story times, about that time
bagpipes shocked the valley. No longer straining
to hear his strains no idea where in the world he is.

Already gone when he came, Bill got only as far
as windows pulling to what I'd have shown him:
the brook and beyond. Studied the fields in their stones
stacked for fires not yet lit for him. Studied the stones
already readying an own flame calling him to island hearth
to build offshore. Saying hello at the same time goodby
I called it, already missing his kindling gifts: Jeffers.
Durrell. How to fight the coal plant coming.

This having menfriends is hard for a Maine raised wife.
If these were women we'd be calling and writing and
coming and going no givings withheld or feared.
Only free gladness for good peers in our time on earth. As is,
I check maps listen to news worry about *the big one*
breaking California, wonder if I'll see his obituary before
one old pal. Imagine Atlantic fires licking salt.

DRESS CODE

in the back pasture
       where
       barely adequate fences
       delineate expectations
is bare
in pinespilled cloth

whatever fur
one wears to the sun
is fine

cow eyes wear us
       swimming in high summer selves
well-bred women gathering
for our mounting gifts
       brimming and considerate
their dreamy watch showing
we know how to behave here
       all tongue and drool

       all graze and cream

SAY THE MEADOW WAS OUR MOTHER

Hadn't I the day before written
to withdraw "What Wealth Can Do"
not wanting that poem to find print
where it might hurt you, known to us only
by what it takes to own ancestral homes, known
to us only as they from away monied people
buying up the coast out of reach to locals, lost
to families but from afar? Now here you are
at the co-op talking Grange and seeds and
back to the land and oh my God when you ask
where home is and we say upriver
but our mother's from the meadow not knowing
it's your meadow and your country-girl hair
echoes your earnest eyes meeting ours
saying your folks were the ones *that makes us*
sisters you lean to an embrace you seem to want
but I don't dare, knowing our place, but
when I let that same want closer
saying what I would give to drink
from my grandmother's spring again
there it wells in your eyes the same as mine.

Loretta! Patricia! Victoria!
Didn't we all have a rich mother
but if we are to walk together
where generations have not, we must step free
from dread, tread with care, feeling
for overgrown fences barbed
with summers worked or played, gates
aged fast against going either way if
we are to honor the womb where muskrats
answer the same water we, and beaver
weave our stories into baskets breathing with truth
knowing better than we where to go from here.

SPECIAL DELIVERY TO PHILIP BOOTH

how long
if I put words to water here
where Shadblow and Trillium improvise
on the side

here brookedge
where deer must wonder *what*
are these new stakes what this cut grass
where we cross

yes
these apple trees sprouted from our scat
no more once you build where we run
another human-claimed place to skirt

how long
if I add my notes to the stream's
will it take to float them to you where you
might wade at Castine

first
slurring north before east again
then south in its own good time
through country left alone a while longer
through towns by people-signs pretending *ours*

leaving me
at Stubbs Brook joining Whites through Duck Cove
to Narramissic down Orland River to the Penob-
scot's eastern channel becoming bay

listen
at Wadsworth shore
where tongues ease in and out on tides with music
I've added message to--Carruth! Can you hear?
I've found Carruth, Booth! *really found*

I send
this news to you where you make poems make jazz
hopin' it tickles your toes in those mudflats knowin'
I've found Carruth no matter
it took so long sometimes like finding you best does

found him
while lookin' for you you know
in that 20th year *Seneca Review*
found you sittin' in with his horn *hey Phil!*
roll up your pants step into my moan
hear me good with those good ears: you guys sure
can play a woman's soul

if I never meet you you good soundin' good men
you'll still be backin' up my blues

GIFTS

Behold
this snow: light
fallen to show us through darkness
toward spring. Please
lift this sighting forward
on worthy words. I
don't know how.
But I believe in you.

HUNGERS AND DAWNINGS
after a particularly long, cold spell

Above snow-sherbeted farm
the moon
a teasing foreign fruit
in a blueberry brandy sky.
East: sunjuice
brimming night's icicled rim.

THE HARD CORE

A tilted house, / a broken back barn /...
Fifty years / I thought I was poor. / But I learned this: /
Good dirt / Is hard to come by.

-- J.B. Goodenough
"Inheritance"

WIND-CHILL FACTOR

                              barriers bound'ries
                         mean nothing these days
                  where things start where
                       things stop
                                 scalding white
            flares across Maine
                  like one forest one
                       field
                                  thrashing
            swirling   spitting
                       as if a wild whining snowwitch
                                      would whirl up
                  from frozen spell curling
                       waves of something shocking
                            scathing
            funneling
                                      shooting
                  on a surface not unlike the sun's
            this one
                       with guts of ice
      solid
      cold

TARPAPER

She's seen the photo: sisters
bundled in wicker carriage in snow
banking little house, pride
of young woodsworking dad. Dodlin Road
West Enfield. Thick black paper
sparkling with grit for siding. It was
what it was: honest. Honorable.

She's seen chapped cheeked kids peeking
through curtains at brave Mama
catching time this once in a camera. Heard
how they got put to bed in snowsuits
against upriver cold, milk freezing
in their bottles. She's walked those woods
where it was, found rusted remains of a bucket
her mother said was their diaper pail and parts
of a pink enamel pot composting
in popple and pine stand. Brought them home
to do something with someday she says.

The town council where she lives now
wants to ban that kind of exterior finish. How'd
you like to have someone build a tarpaper shack
next to you the code enforcement officer
asks her husband.

BEFORE THE BUCKSPORT REGIONAL HEALTH CENTER

Doc Thegen came to the house
when we'd moved downriver
and when we moved outback.
Sat by our beds when our mother needed him.
Delivered the rest of us after the war.
He had a limp, twinkle, and stories to tell
on his calls when people didn't go to hospitals
much. He wouldn't take money
when my father was bad, and he bought
his waiting room magazines from me
so that, altogether, I could win
the basketball and jewelry box at school.
I remember the grand maple chairs
and beaming tile floors and the clock
that showed what time he'd be in.
Sometimes we'd hear a door
on the other side of the house and wonder
about people who lived like that. In town.
Later, he stitched my kid, taking pot roast pay
until things got better.
They named a bridge after him.

SHE CAN COUNT ON TWO HANDS
THE TIMES SHE'S GONE TO A BEAUTY PARLOR
MOST TIMES SORRY SHE DID

Once a week shampoos and for special between
in water lugged from the well, het on the kitchen range.
When someone got headlice most on the schoolbus did. *No disgrace*
to get lice but it's a goddamn disgrace to keep 'em
her father would curse dousing her head with tobacco and kerosene.
Days of nit-picking dread for the school nurse's check
right up and down the aisles for everyone to know. Never enough A's
to cover the shame. Don't look for her to color her hair
her onyx her sterling her leave it alone hair. Do what you want
with yours. She'll tend hers herself, thank you, depending on the flames.

WHEN WINDOWS

If we didn't cover the panes ice did
in sash rotting inches. Tar paper years

then papermachine felt
(what didn't get used on our beds)

over the front door funnel from The North.
Ragged sheep-colored windings hoarded

from the mill still roaring *Saturday Evening...*
and *Life...* wrapping our houses

in scraggly scarfs pounded ritualistically in place
through roughsawn laths each fall. Bits of wool

still surface screaming in cellar-edge soil. Next,
cloudy plastic coverings closed us in. How I wished

to see out our windows all those years dreading
the annual bracing and blanketing that took the light:

the long *out there* light. Now we worship at broad
glass breakthroughs east and south. Even the north,

with lowered case, dares look upon snowheaped nests.
Curtains don't get closed until dark. If then.

HOUSEKEEPING OF A KIND

Once in a great while this house reeks
with remembrances of Wild Rose rage.
The payday cheap gallon kind.
The silent supper kind.
The don't pay any attention to your father
when he's drinking kind.
The fist on the kitchen table pounding kind.
The maybe if I listen he'll like me kind.
The sinks into Kem-tone coverups
and scats along once-a-year-painted
battleship gray, worn to the black,
linoleum floor kind.
The wraps around frozen pipes and spills up
through cracked ceilings
and out leaking roofs kind.
The thirty years later
has to be reminded it was renovated out kind.

Such a stubborn stain.

INCENDIARY

for my papermill overtime working father

She took them to be consultants
when they sat beside her
on the Bangor to Boston flight
discussing "the lesson from Bucksport."
You know, "dialoguing the situation,"
as they say. As they said.

"So what!" one said.
"It was only five thousand and
it was extra anyway."
"Only a perceived loss," one said.
You know, "values" they said.

She strained under her seatbelt
against their sickening tone. Them.
She was a child in the frigid dark carrying
finger biting pails from the well
to the cows, trip after slippery
mitten soaking trip; because
a barge was in and had to be loaded and
it was her father's "value" to work
all the overtime he could get
to make ends meet and
the ends didn't. Meet.

"I hesitate to call it sabotage,"
one said, "but we expected morale
to be improved by now."
"Problem is," one said, "they're reminded
of the cut every week on payday."
"The solution to that is to pay them
once a month," one said
One smiled and said.

She was a teenager being berated
for wanting to accept a party invitation
from friends. Management families.
"Who do you think you are?" her
bitter father instructed.
She hadn't understood.

43

When the pilot announced
changed landing plans,
(out of his hands, he said)
they jostled him through their
textbook talk. Wouldn't want him
working for them, they said.
"Must be a union man," they said.

"Asses!" she wanted to answer,
her smoldering anger threatening
to take them down.
And didn't they think it possible
that union people ever travel
twenty miles upriver, or fly anywhere,
or didn't they care how disgusting
their "dialogue" was in a labor
sympathetic state, or didn't they care
or didn't they care or didn't they care?

Should she call the union? Call
the company? Write letters to the *News*?
She wrote and remembered.
(She'd know where. She'd know
when.) And understood her father
a little better, she said.

HEARING FROM MY FATHER FIVE YEARS DEAD

...but have you noticed / I can't talk about him
without talking like him? --Hayden Carruth, "John Dryden"

DREAM ONE: 8/23/1993
     I suppose I shouldn't be surprised
getting a call from you like that in the night the way
I've been reaching to remember your voice right, how
you sounded, yes, and sayings you passed down
or should I say up to now? Like some godforsaken place
bein' so cold they have to haul the sun in by rope.
Like somebody workin' so hard they're sweatin' like a hen
haulin' cordwood. My sister coming home's helping me remember
and I'm helping her man not resent clover so much, reminding him
that lot's been pasture forever before lawn and giving him
a hard time for calling a field of wildflowers weeds.
     Seemed only right hearing you on the line after listening
to "Eternity Blues" again to put Hayden's sound with his words
put down. Yes, Daddy, Carruth. You may have read him maybe
not, the way you were always picking up poetry books trading
to bring home to Mama. You'd've liked him, too, the way
he writes about the animals and the land and all by seasons
and name, and folks like us and lovings and sufferings and other
reasons for tears (though many a time you told me my bladder's
too near my eyeballs and it doesn't sound any prettier now
than then but look I'm turning it into a poem) and also
through the years: felt music and fun. He'd've thought you
were something, too. Real characters bothofya.
     Reminds me how you and Narnie Cole use'ta chew the fat
swearin' how whichever went first would come back to spook
the other. And how you'd tell that story he told you how
when he was sellin' milk to the county creamery and they
allowed as how the bacteria count was too high he'd slat a fistful
of disinfectant powder into every can before poundin' the cover
down. *There! That'll take care of the goddamned bacteria.*
     Hey, Hayden's all right. He's walked our walk and he sure knows
our talk except he's not against as many as you were.
Why he's written with heart so many times he thought
he should write a poem apologizing for it. Tried to figure that out
all these years how comin' up the way you did you could look down
on any. If we had hard words it was over that and how all I ever
wanted was to believe you prized or even liked me the way I tried
to prize and like you trying to understand coming up so hard

made it so hard for you to show love the way a daughter needs.
But that song's an old rag and those blues can get along without me.
        Come morning--well you know how dreams feel so real so
long--I swear you sounded glad to reach me. And even if your words
faded soon as said, I got to tell you we've missed you, then when
I asked you something I can't remember for the life of me
you were gone. But I still feel loved by that call however it came.
I needed to feel valued some by you, too, reading how Hayden
could say he appreciates something about the woman I've been
knowing me only through a few small poems
but it was so hard for you to and it's goin' on forenoon and I'm still
holding these meanings to me weeping pleasure's pain, grateful
as this dried up old summer for any measure of rain.

DREAM TWO: 8/29/1993
        I'm watching a truck delivering oil to my mother
where we used to live over back in Millvale. The place
you bought on the GI Bill after the war. I begin to worry about her
seeing the driver go inside. You're on the phone again.
How're you doing I must have asked. All right.
I've got a job but it don't pay like the one I used to have.
We always managed to....   What? *What!*
Get by? Make it? Don't cry *yes we did yes we did.*

        She's working with a hammer in an upstairs hall
in that old house that filled with water to the top
of the cellar stairs every spring built in that wet valley
like that. There's been a renovation. Fine molding.
Carpet. Big closet she always wanted but never had.
More like the house she grew up in, the house
I just heard my son sold marble to. The house
I've written about trying to keep in memory. *Don't worry*
I'm doing just great! she yells she never asked for carpets
or fancy woodwork just a good sized closet would've pleased.

        My father's gone. Did I tell you when he was little
he had to wear a bag of skunk oil around his neck to ward off
the croup? Did I tell you Mama still has the invitation
to the inauguration of Ed Muskie they got for helping elect
the first Democratic governor in the State of Maine in years
and at a time you were pretty much told working at the mill
which way you were expected to vote? It's in one of those shoe
boxes in the corner of the back room where she keeps what's left
of his stuff. It's not the skunk fat that stinks most you know.

46

WHY I DON'T NEED MUCH

Because Great Grandmother Myra's
husband fetched her a dress a year
on his trips to trade or shoes
if she really needed those.
All he needed to know
was her size.

Because Grandmother Hattie
wore cotton dresses until
they frayed through
where she rubbed against her work
in front then patched them and
covered them with aprons worn too
and patched.

Because my mother
never needed anything
she could do without.

WATER!

...and the holy wonderness of water when it does come,
the relief of water, when it comes, the slap on the back,
the giddy whoooooooooosh, the mess, the hustle.

--Carolyn Chute, *Merry Men*

Today's the day: August 4 1990. Word is passed
both sides pace waiting out the labor watching
in shifts for clay to let up life.   How

     deep

     now

     how

     much

     longer?

Hours listening for liquid on seared soil ledge. Men
women kids pass beer lemonade lean on trucks
follow shadepatch around young house.

     20

     feet

     44

     drill

     pierces

     rock

     wails

     across

     valley

then there it is at a hundred and sixty *2 gallons a minute!*
Two hundred and four gives six! Panning for wealth
men measure flow and pasture runs wet in a new place.

     We've

     got

     water!

Word is passed to generations wanting the news the grand-
mother yells as if it's her own still carrying lugging water
in jugs in frayed cloth sacks she made for the job years
ago she knows water's worth. While others envy riches
of another kind she marks the day her grandaughter's well
comes in says if she's ever to be interested in another man
he'll have to have plenty.   Water.

     Water!

When the call comes she cheers as if they've struck oil
diamonds gold. Same thing.

PEDIGREES

In mansions called cottages
grander than any she'd seen
she did their laundry and tended
their kids between waiting on.
Crumbed their tables. Served lemoned
fingerbowls on doilied plates.

At a hotel called a house
grander than any she'd seen
her tips turned tuition
to upriver halls and
a second generation Berkshire boy
whose grandfather laid up
Lake Como stone, brought rock-wall lyrics
to his new world.

Now for estates called places
grander than any he's seen
her son makes island granite gardenworks
and Italian marble boards, polishing
with diamond grit.

She cleaned up after them. Her son
creates their surrounds. She, anonymous,
instructed not to converse. He
leaves his mark in their stone.

LET NO WORD ASK TO NAME THIS

in the stall next to ours
Blue Hill Fair

scrubbed
polished and
groomed
thoroughbred cow
papers to show
eyes wide choking
WILL A VET
PLEASE REPORT
TO THE CATTLEBARN
arms thrust down throat
pitchfork-handle prod
whatever might budge
that cud *my god* nothing
would *nothing*
eyes wide knife
through hide see
that ball of hay
that boss hoisted
by bucket-loader waved
from sawdust pile
braided tail
buffed hoofs and horn
hoisted and gutted
and skun for meat
just like that
just as plain and
just as fast and
with no more words
than this either

BUCK PASSING

Crack of rifleshot shocks them upright
in more darkness than dawn the kick stinging the spools
of their half a century of hunting seasons bed,
                              Holy God!
their good morning. A pickup pulls from below their room
the better to load. Across the road neighbors figure
he must have shot from the cab. Across the brook
families watch. Through doors overlooking the run
they stare in silence to see the Majesty of The Valley
                              The Prince
whose vision became theirs whenever they turned
from the ledgeroad home after dark always with herd
head high with bone.
                              The Crowned One
whose hoofs have signed the land deep marking *mine*
roped like a steer dead weight dragged
over seed-spilling field up gravel bank over his own tracks
forever gone.
                              Bastard!
Shot too close to the house as if being illegal it might not be true.
They could have stayed in bed it was over so fast stayed
under the woolen blanket with four point stripes selvage side
showing how many fine pelts would have fetched it in fair trade
years ago stayed under brandied mincemeat stocking overhead beams.
                              Nights after
the does are watched waiting in the fields. Hunting's different
when it's someone you know a daughter says and NO HUNTING
signs go up both sides never posted before. They still tell
of the taking at the Rod & Gun Club up the road.

FIRST SNOW

for a daughter divorcing

And isn't it true:
what didn't get done
doesn't matter anymore. Buried.
That's all she wrote your grandfather
would say about things being over. Some
things can't be saved. Uncle George says

the doe seen crossing has twins,
says she comes regularly by the barn.
He's seen her rear up on hind legs,
hoof the air, her fawns following,
learning whatever it is she's teaching.
What *National Geographic* would give
to have that if only he could've gotten it
on film. Imprints

of all our winters expose an annual ache
for what we can't name but are pulled by.
To windows. To fields. To woods.
To remembered good and grief. The truth
of seasons, what it means: something else
ending. Rise up to the cold. Sense for signs.
The way to go. Your instinct for spring.

HARD FROST

For Carolyn Schelling, whose exquisite short season
left us applauding through tears.

Don't think
    Rugosa: because
    you've been brought in
    to bouquet breakfast, keep company
    with tea and toast, their warmth will
    save you even with that bud
    still a hope that is only a folded point
    proving we all die with the wholeness
    of all we can be still in small promises
    showing;

    Nasturtium: because
    your watermelon orange lemon lips
    sing choral color into morning sun
    beaming heat through saving glass past crown
    of thorns four-feet-of-seasons tall, scented
    geraniums lifting to the bright through
    brilliance-blue violet, jungles and oceans
    from home, African petals storing specks of shine,
    you can winter with them you can't, your hours
    counted;

    Delphinium: because
    you managed a late last spike
    when we needed you blue in the yard
    that earns you eternity, though you're certainly
    dressed for the occasion little ladder
    of skydrops trying to get back up budding
    as tall as it takes.
    Sorry.

Surely you all must know
if we could make it so you'd go on. Wouldn't
we mess things up and would we adore you the same
were you here all year and what about God.

But Rose: having been robbed of your right
to live on in citrus-hip oaths, I vow to save
you in sweet smelling jar to be remembered
for what you are what you've been.
Forgive.

And Nasturtium: your vased cressleaves fading
in here, your stoneside patch frozen dead
out there, will it be enough to know
your glow is so necessary seeds will be sought
every year to bring you back?
We will!

And Del: don't worry.
Your mother's safe in earth's living arms. When
you rise into spring you'll find good family again
more of you cherished in gratitude each year
thanking you for showing *up.*

AFTER THE THANKS GIVING
OR
WHEN MOTHERS DIE TOO YOUNG

for Carolyn's boys

Lost to words to map
this kind of grief this
coldest winter coming, she turns
to a crash on the bulkhead. A red
applebomb bursts, shatters her core
when she spies high in the locust
from which it dropped heavy,
the small one on its own now
mornings after the mother shot
by the farmer watching his store
disappearing daily, squirreled
from shed to hedgerow hands;
by the farmer fearful of chewed wire
fire. Her hope for young ones shaken,
all she knows is their sky is falling
                    their sky *is* falling.

FOR MINNIE BOWDEN

Once in great whiles
a woman long here uncovers a power
passed down like live coals fire to fire
a few true fish being enough to marvel her
people from starving for their own tongue they never
thought they'd hear raised again except as joke. Forbidden,
sung in the woods on their holy days, a scarce oil
no one would believe could sustain their scattering remainder
of inherited, *for wilderness, for lost*, light. Writing alone
with scant expectation for inclusion in gatherings professing
to speak this place, local women learn to burn theirs
into fibers from own pressings, till them into *for giving*
gardens from which once in great whiles
an eloquent slip is bestowed
but only to a safe knowing few
and quietly.

TEACHING ME

Is this the rime
you wrote you saw
crossing New Hampshire's grain,
that mountain cold moved
down east to Maine? Down
to my view nothing to do
with me: here or not,
this will be. Selfish
to imagine these flashes most
call diamonds could be tears.
Neither science nor any other truth
will have any of that. Nor those
bound by *real*. Phenomenologically,
however, I know it's up to me.
If I see ice drops caught fast
in gardens, vast fields and woods,
it's because I need them
to have frozen there where
they may have fallen from gods
and souls who give a damn
so mine won't seem so many.
Or few. So I may know.

HARKING

Each singing what belongs to him or her and to none else.
--Walt Whitman, "I Hear America Singing"

OUTBACK WOMAN

sometimes I urge to back up   out more   back more
where a woman can put tarpaper on a shed
and not be less

carry pails from untested springs
squat where she wants and not break codes

dress nothing like the ads and not worry
some domesticated souls'll drive in not knowing
where in hell they're at

eat from the rough follow rhythms   signs
primal sense my clock

in the shock of wild juice remember everything
about how I've been there before

FOR THE LOVE OF LEARNING

for Hattie

Sorting junk mail piled for days on dining room table
last two almost thown unopened but one
was from Union River Fabric and *liquidation* caught my eye
like maybe there were bargains to be had, you know
what a softie I've always been for deals on cloth
you'd be proud bits of yours still saved. Closer to trash

than that came a piece from UM computer labeled
must be for money. Curiosity nothing more saved it:
In recognition of your superior academic
achievement...members of Phi Kappa Phi extend
an invitation.... honest to God. Must've been that 4 point
I got that year I thought I should dare do a doctorate
even if I had to settle for half way, mind willing body not.
Honest to God, Mamie, what would you think?

Made a good big pea soup for supper. Biscuits in the oven
even as I write. My own *receipt* isn't that how your
generation said it? Olive oil instead of leaf lard now
no animals left except chickens, no heavy chores to keep
hearts safe. Mamie: I promise you I scooped flour
from the family tin under the sideboard and the sifter
handed down. Soured milk myself with vinegar no clabber
thickening on the woodstove either something had to give.

Mamie: I've done my best and hold it up to you hoping
you'd think so knowing how times have changed. I know
you'd be proud of my stitchery and cookery
and about Phi Kappa Phi I think you'd say *ayeah?* on an
indrawn breath almost too soft to hear the *That so?*
Good for you dear I'd know you'd mean. Not sloppy
and dumbsounding like comics making fun of us
but lady-like in our own way of talking and knowing. All
these degrees Mamie and all I want to do is study you in me
get it down so's it'll be there real and true beside writers
from away making up theirs. Help me remember. Put it right.

AMY CLAMPITT SHOWIN' ME WHO I AM
AT FRASER'S AUTO SALES AND SERVICE
STOCKTON SPRINGS, MAINE, MARCH 1990

Seen your name in *Poets & Writers* and so forth so
waitin' for my mother's wagon I was some glad to find that 12/4/89
New Yorker in the pile with *Motor Magazine, Wooden Boat,*
Fiji's gift catalog, *Sears Home Catalog, People Magazine*
and a *Yankee* with the poetry page gone. Your poem
caught my eye 'cause I thought I should know what kind of stuff
you write. So after checkin' the cartoons--seen that one where
the jacket's honkin', called "The goose down acts up?"--I read
"A Note From Leiden." Kinda hard figurin' out what you were
writin' about and I just had the time it took for an oil change,
grease job, filter, and tirecheck. They specialize in cars under 2000
so they're real busy and have to work fast.

Pleasant enough place to pass the time with your poem. Free coffee
and gum-ball machine of chocolate covered raisins for those so inclined.
"Butts Please" and "No Car No Cash" signs keep things in order.
Got to expect some grit from garage work and gravel driveway
comin' into pot hole time. Thought those posters advertisin' Mega-tron
batteries and Acousticat Catalytic Converters were tricky, but when I got
home had to look up "polder," "fleche," and "tumid," though I figured tumid
might have been like the proprietor's goose got before she laid that first egg
his wife came in to tell us about. "Guess that means mud season's comin,"
she said and "guess we won't open the restaurant
'til the end of May this year.
Cold without heat."

Bangor Library says there's a Leiden in the Netherlands. Guess
you must've taken a trip and it rained hard in the night. That it?

NON SCRIVERÒ

I will not write to tell you
> how I've changed some points of view, seen other angles
>> in what I've written before
> how I wish I could rewind time to the place my words
>> made you ask for more to teach to: dreaded treasured (re)marks
> how I've got Murray, Millay, Haxton, Moore, Jeffers, Auden,
>> Strand stacked for study, stacked against you
> how it comes to me when I read: I must remember to mention
>> this
> how new paths and views take me inevitably to wanting
>> to let you know
> how journals and reviews test and tease me to tell you
>> remembering how you were glad with my graspings
> how I want to ask you questions for the longed for pleasure
>> of your replies
> how ice-out at the pond came April 5th this year although
>> it was a good two weeks before the final turning
> how snowdrops are blossoming under the plum tree, daylilies
>> pointing green by the pear
> how my people call these stubborn late-spring snowfalls
>> poor man's fertilizer
> how I still, yes, fight to find words to write the pain, doubt
>> and joy you helped me own
> how I'll hold to knowing your hope for me, your belief
>> bracing mine
> how I'm pushing to remember you're expecting copies
>> of my proudest work in print
> how my grandboy now says dada in Hall's sweetful milk-tongue
>> and takes a few steps daring to stand alone
> how I'm daring to stand alone missing a poetry teacher
>> I never had now you've shown me how a good one can be
> how I feel spoiled not wanting another polestar
>> knowing you this way this brief life space
> how it always boils down to mastering the letting go
>> so

I will not write to tell you
> how much I want to write to tell you

SOURCES

First find violets, wild,
last of May. in Maine when bees
are working blueberry bells and hummingbirds
everything bright.

Next find white vinegars, wine,
for the color to infuse and show. *Dal Raccolto*
from Tuscan vines or *Saveurs de France* from Champagne.

Pick a teacup deepest purple keeping petals or whole.
Inspect for insects (a matter of taste). No need
to rinse after rain and pollen adds to the prize. Carefully

pull off each calyx (they seep green)
and drop into vinegar of choice recapping tightly
and overturning several times to immerse. Seal
in plastic wrap to keep out dust, let in light, and set
in sun-catching place about a month following warmth
in windows east to west (cold springs) for color
and oils to work, tipping to mix when memory occurs.

Tag reverently and give to someone
deserving or needing heaven's essence on earth.
Be sure to make one to keep for darkest winter depths.
For sacraments of survival and celebration.

To make *violet vinaigrette* shake in screwtop jar:
2 teaspoons sugar, white or brown, or honey half as much
half teaspoon mustard, dry
clove garlic, crushed
3 tablespoons this vinegar
9 tablespoons good olive oil or nut. Will keep.

To make *creamy violet vinaigrette*:
beat 3 tablespoons cream or yogurt
with 6 tablespoons this *viola vinum*. Will not keep.

Elegant on light salad leaves and white fish dishes.
Remember to taste for voice.

TO SHARON BRAY

Never mind dandelion greens,
rhubarb pie, next load of wash ready to hang
to dry in shadtree petalfall. This Moment, these sheets
with word designs are all: poems from you
I never knew put down poems. Now

here they are another fresh flock of song come
this Canada-goose-on-the-pond morning
(oh no has it lost its mate) this hummingbird-
in-the-tulips day this swallow-sweeping week
this chicken-setting month this don't-we-all-
need-to-nest season while

over in Troy they're sowing a new Maine book
not even knowing about you. You haven't
asked/allowed...for years, you say, for any
reading, now these notes thrilling me. My cousin:

your verses feel as real to all I've known
as other life discovered by track and call now your
secret prints have made their way outback this way
your rhythms tonic to this weather-beaten heart. What artful
sense you leave here passing: deer in fog and under oak,
and other creatures habiting this place, and kinfolk spirits
gone before some long some a yesterday we can't believe
is a longer time than we'll allow. How
can I thank you but to hold your writings to me
taking them to be, as for you, bloodlines. Roots.

SWAPPING
OR
WHY I LOVE GROWING OLD OUT BACK

because when my old man
finished closing in the new shed
and called me to come see
we looked at each other and giggled
and he said he'd give me
a couple strawberries if I would
I lifted my skirt
and we laughed like hell

PASTORALE

Hancock Pond
East Bucksport

If you've come upon it where Route 46 curves
down from Dedham or out from town

at the Hewey Town Road crossing, you'll remember:
black and white holsteins graze and gather

in pasture licked eternally by a sudden small pond,
its springfed surface a silver wine shining in the sun, water

reeds Edening its edge. Waders and swimmers know
its sediment's a muck of mysteries and memories feeding

water purer than most called holy. You'll remember
it bathes ledged footings of an aged church whose knotty

neighbors and pine cross hold on ruggedly against fears
they can't earn their keep. You know their kind. Too few left.

Closest thing to a stable site come to think of it especially
haying time. Perfect testament and psalm. Why you'd swear

angels of the north must sing: *Look here, God! Look here!*
And that pretty pond warm or white is a baptismal font

of the finest kind for those who know a good-enough
heaven when they see one.

AFTER BROOKLIN BENEDICTION

Now I lay me down to sleep
having finally washed Eggemoggin brine
from my face. Mussel supper at midnight
to sanctify the day. Sweet meat shelled
in blue-black pearl opening
to cleansing broth steaming
under seaweed gathered in baby's pail
along the cove. Past E.B. White's white place
then Amen Farm and Allen families
there long as any still there.

Didn't that artist
take a radiant canvas home today
and boaters, fishers, and tourists own
salt views. I know I still see
my grandchild prizing life's first feather
out to me. *Tetty?* Oh, yes! *Pretty!*
Tickling his cheek then mine. His. Mine.
But a snatching breeze blows the new thing
from his hand twirling it beyond surprise,
tiny fluff of a dreidel dancing out of sight
out to sea.

May this Mainechild, too,
keep this day well, store this place
to come back to, perhaps, I pray,
in an art of his own. And yes:
Amen.

NOT FAR FROM THE COAST: AUGUST: MAINE

Tansy time.
Bare feet
      in early day dew, cool.
Wet webs in needles and thorns and grass
      signal one of those heavy hot days
      when the sun burns off.
Robin lets them have a turn at highbush fruit,
      baby dropping berries to cup
      then one by one reaches for ones
      to chew, his yearling eyes as big as blue
      as the cultivated gems coloring his world
      new. As if that's where the idea came from.
Ripe fog sags into soup
      dripping from plum tree leaves.
The grandmother can't think
      of a single place she'd rather be
      than with this child in this garden
                  in this time.
In savory haze
      she drinks this morning for breakfast.

REAPING

for W

Come down to the island I'll take you out
he calls upcountry from Northeast. All you need's warm clothes
weather and tide being right come down. Old friends different paths.
There in memory the stirring of something shared to taste again.
So they leave their garden the urgency of harvest before frost
for afternoon on the coast. Last blueberries still to be raked.

Potatoes still in the ground. Summer crops begging for freezer
and jar. A day too long their winter store gone the killing moon
coming full. In precious hours they put work aside how often
does a call like this come. They pack a sack and drive south guessing
what to wear to sea. Off Clifton Dock 'round the privileged
point they board his Sea Hawk heading out.

Saluting luxury class and working craft both his boat a cross be-
tween he navigates past acres of cultivated wealth to free Atlantic
air. Sea-fowl country. Osprey roost worthy to be measured in cords
piled on rockjut the rust of their old John Deere. The sort of headpiece
God would wear more nest than crown so majestically woven and
watched over so capable of life. And holding court belted king-

fisher and heron the color of weather-endured stone.
Cormorants. Guillemots. Why he'd fly and dive too if he could
she knows creature of sea as much as land. Not his fault
he doesn't have wings or gills. Still he swims with seals in channels
he knows by soul I can get most places they can his creed. There
Baker Island yes of the Gilley family tale about locals loved

for tending summerpeople by boat good weather and foul
but she sees it another way remembering the old man lost his life
rowing milk for children of the rich lost to his kin so they could stay on
into fall faithful servant he was. She sees it another way having done
her time in that service years ago. To Bunker Ledge and its East
to watch for seals. White-tail deer on Sutton heading back. Sailboats.

Water limos. Magnificent Friendship sloop. Each vessel a story
like us he says. Motor off they float to the sun touching in from the west
giving his tanned skin to glow. Face muscles as familiar with expressions
of risk and reward as he with their place on the chart. Baseball.
Children. Remembrances. Hopes. They toast this test of who
they are now with raspberry wine and beer. She watches

their handsome back-and-forths and wants to break in with a *hey!*
seeing three spirits rise clasp hands and dance showing those seals
a thing or two. Wants to splash into their stories *come on let's play!*
Instead hearing of knots and splices and whatnot sees bell-bottoms
pea coat. A sailor's smile. Tells her dad was a rigger and bosun's
mate in Two. God those guys were legends he cheers and she

salts away her saved jig with preserved tears for the ripeness of it all.
Next day home boiling jars making dills what're you thinking
he wants to hear. About yesterday. Something happened out there
in that boat. What do you mean? Something you men didn't know.
What. I saw us all hold and dance. Why didn't you say
something Christ you know we would've.

SEPTEMBER STAYING

The air is made of missing:
spaces where you were, sounds
lacking yours. A robin basks
on the arbor appreciating as much
as I and whole bubbles of butterflies
bounce in the garden quiet but for
crickets nearby, crows far off,
leaves high up. Certain flies buzz
somewhere. The spider still weaves
in the hops vine but hummingbirds
have gone, like summerfolk, like you,
to other worlds leaving hardy ones
to season ourselves in stillness again
to find our own peace. Our own place.

HOLDING

Autumnal Equinox
Bucksmills Road

Under skies approaching Bangor International Airport
upriver 20 miles, less as the crow flies, where planes
bank wide waiting to land, I drag a chair
from wellhouse to sheltered spot of sun

under the old Mac by the woodpile facing south.
Drops turn beezy in hawkweed grass even
as I write. Goldenrod nod their facts of life
and lavender whispers from wild asters wave "That's right!"

This valley's produced fruit to spare for Polly Bishop's
crabapple jelly and Mary Gross's green tomato relish
and I, myself, would be glad to show you my latest elder-
berry jam and tell you intentions to put up more,

God knows, than I'll get done. But just this moment
between sweat and shiver won't you linger
with me and admire Earleen Clement's winter squash, how
they're swelling along that vine like new generations

building on family land all along this road. Sure
it's clouding over and will be darkening toward nightfall
soon, that jet's going the way of whole flocks,
it's getting chilly and my flannel shirt's inside. Still....

still....before I turn to build the fire these chickadees
tell me I must, wait with me and take in summer's
ripest hours to save. Breathe in and keep well
her smell. Now hurry along to put harvest soups to boil,

oatmeal cookies for kids back to school. Don't forget
to come back out to cover tender beds
and last cukes with tablecloths and sheets
before dark. Tonight could be the night.

MARK THIS DAY WITH CANDLE AND SONG

October 1, 1993

And it's snowing slow locustleaf flakes
this morning to the full harvest moon.

Have you heard the coal plant people
have given up plans to build in the cove?

Squirrels! Heave this victory with cranberries
and pears up that tree and chatter the news

down hedgerows that all nests may know
and call--*no, sing!*--down burrows and dens

then to the pond that perch and hornpout may catch
and dive the meaning to all preparing for ice, pure

creature-joy spilling over to brook where deer and bear
will drink something glad not knowing what.

SERVICE AT SILVER LAKE

Oh don't expect me to write spare
in all this glory please. Bare is for November.
And winter. Not this here and now, these
feather-gold leaves lifting off birch, flocking north
as if forgetting to head south or simply fall.

This rowboat drifting into the hush
past beaver lodge to pine-walled cove where
cattails crewel the banking's cuff and water-
rubbed roots braid a band. How can I write plain
this meadowgrass collar still green to the shore

laced with the forest's shadowy shawl? Not
elaborate on heron and duck honoring Silveridge Farm,
its contoured procession of berrycloth gowns marching
sweet memories of first fruits gone to apples
praising upper fields? I think it good

to notice woods are wearing the make-up
of ripe garden skins: butternut ash, buttercup spruce.
Blue hubbard here. And there: carrots and corn.
Beet-red! To echo on paper whole stands repeating
the harvest's circumstance and pomp. Before promising

to embroider less my way of saying
I beseech you to notice how, having crowned
this season with vestments befitting the rite,
the sun gathers her dress from across
the water and bows below the holy horizon west.

SINGERS

You should hear my new tapes
my mother sings primo to my girl. *One's Swiss yodelin'*
and two oboe.

> *Take these,* her oboe-major grand-
> daughter joins: *Ronstadt*
> *doing the big band sound, songs of the 40s*
> *and so forth. And here,*
> *with Parton and Harris.*

If I had it to do over I'd be a singer. Instruments
are good but when it's your own voice they's no
other sound like it in the whole world. Don't
give up your singin' will you dear. I used to sit in
with my father on cornet and played piano for dances
with my brother George on bass and Oscar Butler
on drums. They's nothin'
like bein' in a good band is they.

FOR A NEW NEW YEAR'S MORNING

Sun-swell down and east
from Great Pond Mountain
is an ocean of coming up light. Night
an ebbing tide with shoresong
sure as any. Our woodlot-top a coast

to an inland miraging sea. Day a rising bay
so fluid lobster boats could haul traps from it
on lines dripping with freezing salt.
That black fir spire could be a steeple
crackling over a town tucked around ice-

bound cove. Those flat-bottomed clouds: islands
fast as Mount Desert under snow. See
how first light gives new dreams
through old growth pine. An ocean
needs only to be wished for; conjured,

any sea can be. Dawn washes
the waking pasture flooding on
to become its own day. You'd never know
the Atlantic breaks outback each sunreach
unless as I do, you believe.

ANSWERING HOW COME YOU ALWAYS
ROCK THE BABY

Because I read him a poem through your mama's skin about coming out
    when he was still in her baby-growing place
because I was happy when I heard he was coming and I'm glad he's here
    like you.
Because I paced, too, waiting and wanting him born.
Because I held him minutes into the world and whenever I could after
because I'm his grandmother and want him to know what I feel like
    and sound like and smell like so he'll know me the way I know him.
Because he rocked in warm water in your mama's womb and misses it
    and because she likes to rock him, too, and I can help.
Because for more hundreds of thousands and thousands of hundreds of years
    than we can count, people have liked rocking children so much
    they have made all kinds of wonderish roundish carriers to rock
    them in. You know: cradles and swings and animal seats with springs,
    back and forth chairs and to and fro toys that tip and then come back
    again (*See-saw, Margery Daw....!*).
Because I have a lap and arms and a chair on rockers, see how it's made.
Because rocking's what we're supposed to do with babies
because all creatures of the earth who know enough curl around their new
    ones and cuddle them with safe sounds like *urrrr* and *umf umf umf*
    and *kooooo* and whatever sounds they make to mean: you
    are our baby and we love you.
Because hearing *loo loo loo lye* and *la la la lay* he'll hear how sounds
    make meanings and like to hear *lily*, and other flower names and
    linger, which means stay awhile and he might, and *Lilliputian*
    meaning very small things he might want stories about.
Because my mama and daddy taught me rocking songs their
    mamas and daddies taught them like *Too-ra-loo-ra-loo-ral...* and
    I had a little doggy that used to sit and beg... and
because we want to teach new children in our family
    so you will teach yours.
Because I gave birth to his father and sang these lullabies to him and
because rocking his baby's like rocking him again.
Because I sang these songs to you when I met you and you were two and
because I would have rocked you when you were a baby if you
    were in our family then and
because I would rock you any time you want me to now
because the time you little ones want to be rocked is so short isn't it.

Because no matter how old we get a few rocks a day help keep the blues
    away;
because even when we're grown we like to hold, *la la lee*,
    and be held, *la la lye*, and remember how like a lullaby
    it feels to move in someone's arms like Grampa holds me,
    and we sway, *la la lay!* in our own rocking way,
    and call it dancing.

TO CASTINE QUIETLY

for Bennett Dunbar

Hush there where Lowena Devereaux sells ice creams
on her porch there where you'll decide to bear west
around Morse's Cove where families dig clams for canners
hissing with seaweed boiling over

onto sand, or stay straight ahead down hardwood road
watching where old maples hold over the curve. Hark
for gravel's crunch. For stable floorboards answering steps.
For the drinking-dipper sinking back

into springwater bucket on the bench there where the screen door
sings open, claps shut. *Sing!* Clap. *Sing!* Clap. Inside,
gullcall of handpump lifting cistern rain
from cellar to slate to eternal flame.

Someone's appendix burning in the stove.
The *clock----clock, clock----clock* pendulum marking time
to this day. Mind you the children overheard overhead tumbling
into featherbed play and woodpeckers

working their meadow below. Duncan Dunbar pulling out chairs
for Hattie. Others, after, pulling up theirs. His long
silent treatment for a sister who dared wear pants
to hay in. Hear ice-cutting years

and pleasures with pung there where firetrucks fill. Quiet
for Clara West lifting pantry latch and lids from crocks blessing cookies
to offneck kids. For her web-still thread
through a sewing bird's beak there

on her worktable upstairs over Bagaduce dream. *Shshsh*
for Annie Lou and Jean stealing bareback races on pastured mares.
Catch them laughing still, free from pain again. Tinpail bales chiming
with climbers lunching up in that storied tree

there by that wooden school. Heed one room warmed and worn.
Hearken for the place the village begins. For a sculptor tearing away
what's in the way of what he hears. For pens
weeping poems into night.

CLAIMING

She could imagine living here
as her mother did time ago
down the road apiece, only she'd
tear out the wall-to-wall, bring back

old fixtures and floors. Call it *Tall Oaks*.
Take an upstairs room facing east out
over the orchard, the salt slope
to Warm Cove warm enough weathers.

Cold, she'd come down to woodstove
writing flicker of Maine to flame. Write
the hot cheeks of her mother's youth
when a boy on Wardwell Point

asked which one she'd like and gave her
her own island when the bay was world,
theirs to bestow and receive. Like stars:
Which one? It's yours. Offneck girl

courted in outback fields she'd have
swapped gladly to be in town. Declining
to look into windows of time, this house
for sale, she stays in the car, daughter

sailing view to view refusing to keep
her place. Pulls a grapevine slip gone wild
to bury inland, upriver, back home.
Samples each tree: *Oh, these! These!*

Refusing what apples could mean again
the mother dreads what her daughter
might expect next. Scanning offshore
with a want she can taste:

Which one's ours, Mama? Which one?

CALLS

Calls are usually simple notes, single or repeated, given
at all seasons to express alarm or to maintain contact...
Above all, listen.
　　　　　　--Familiar Birds of North America, Eastern Region

Indelible the day Castine pulled
saying what, I'd no idea
nor would I have gone
had I known. We took tea
to the backshore where Winter
was turning
and breaking up into great
beached slabs
and the Penobscot's eastern basin
filling with day going down.
We harkened to that sacred still
until a car kept scalloping ours
watching as if we were up to no good.
Someone's caretaker taking
good care no doubt.
　　　　　　　　　Never mind
　　　　　　　　　never mind

an old spirit-kin signed.

　　　　　　　　　You come
　　　　　　　　　you come.
　　　　　　　　　Come.

So we moved on down the peninsula
intending to drive straight to the wharf
when a different force cried No.
Not turn down Main Street
in my people's town? Night nothing
compared to that fall, all meanings
still fogged in new ghostly tone until
detouring to the dock's cold shoulders
I saw: *our Castine is gone*: my
truth not an island offshore but a stone
in Bagaduce ground.
　　　　　　　　　Go home.
　　　　　　　　　Go home.
　　　　　　　　　Lest McCarthy's specter appear

or you should meet Hardwick's
high wand
and you there
on their side Route One.

Yes, yes,
up One sixty-six
Mamie's place
will assuage never mind
never mind don't
look.
Don't look.

My pen shudders to hold what can't be kept.
How the stable's been sleighted
by modern and good intentions to nothing our
heritage can own.

Gone... gone... gone.

Gone Dearest Door to floorwood
still capable of echoing our songs. Gone fragrance
from Dunc's worn tools for longing for forging
for sweating a way to live. No
call but gone true enough
still to honor, I bow to try:
the passage to our being in time boarded now:

Goodbye
then *goodbye*
and *goodbye.*

I wish to go back to before I knew

or never go back at all.

QUEST: FOR JOHN ANDREWS CALLED OLD BUCK

1.

Reaching for you I remember Penobscot lullabies I don't remember
    from that winter boarding with you when my father
    worked for your chief. Through my mother's womb
    I heard you singing to my sister you were rocking
    and I wanted to be born to you.

2.

Believing you my mother stopped being afraid I'd come in a storm
    marooning caretakers on the lake. Comforting her
    you comforted me now 54 years more I still will
    to hear you croon *Medicine Man*
    last full-blooded member to your band
    the moccasin maker told me buying snowy ones
    to surprise my mother's leather heart.

3.

Calling you there's a sweetgrass braid nailed by the door
    to our house   herbs
    drying in the entry   jars filled with forest scents.
    Baskets some might think I collect.

4.

Following you I save feathers
    so when my nephew came from the West
    and we took him to Orono's show up Your River
    then to Your Island Left   told him
    what he needed to know so when he wanted
    to make me a talking stick like one he saw there
    I had cedar waxwing red-tipped and yellow-edged
    as though dipped in blood in sun   partridge
    striped and goose grey and white
    and also from my store cotton floss stained deep
    for fingerweaving rounds with rawhide we found
    to go with hedgerow wood he gave up TV to cut.

5.

Due to you I crave shells
   more than coin didn't I stitch them
   to a skin-trimmed dress with stones
   for The USAs celebration of when it thought
   this country was old? Colonial costumes
   for husband and kids made authentic as I could
   but I would wear my Eastern Woodland design   studied
   embroidered   imagined to be true   to honor you.

6.

Envisioning you an ash box for picnics centers our times on Your Shores.
   Gift from the Mitchell Clan's George   *a bear*
   whose forgiveness came to me in a dream.

7.

Hearing you I could forgive the professor good man white too
   who expected me to fit his script
   for what whites think about tribes. He knew
   what he knew from his statistical search but nothing
   from the way it was with us no sense
   trying to get through he was an expert he had a grant.

8.

Because of you my children know how being here longer sometimes
   only means our people were guiltier at first some the whole time
   but now how the circle having started around back then
   is coming around again our people being pushed from the land
   though that doesn't give us the right to say we know why you cry.

   I've taught it and written it what little it counts.
   Will anyone care if I tell Castine their four flags logo is wrong
   their *Battle Ground of Four Nations* motto forgetting *The First*
   there's still time before Their Bicentennial to save
   themselves saying that joke   like Bucksport at Theirs
   claiming their founder built the river's first boat?

9.

Learning you I study Alexie
   his <u>Business of Fancydancing</u>   <u>First Indian On the Moon</u>
   imploring him to bleed more fire that we might burn
   for the joy he calls himself *Skin.*
   Take English tea barefooted to rocks   wish
   to die outside needing no higher heaven.

10.
Holding to you I make love with the earth,

11.
holding to you and The Nation's Nicola boys she made fudge for
    those howling nights playing 83.   Not trying
    to steal any soul John Andrews called Old Buck only save
    what you gave wanting us to have   give
    something back join the walk long.
                        In silence
I seek your spirit John Andrews called Old Buck

and concentrate to know what you would want me to know
about not being afraid.
About song.

12.
                            Seeking you.

NOTES

"In Their Dust": The second edition of *The Gray Family of Hancock County, Maine* (cited in epigraph) tracing descendants of George and Sarah Gray from the Kittery-Berwick region from 1659, then from the Castine peninsula from 1761, was compiled by Almon A. Gray and Walter A. Snow in 1987 and is available through the Castine Historical Society.

"What The Fields Know": *ONTHEBUS*, the title of a literary journal out of Los Angeles, signifies the counter-culture movement of the 1960s in which buses and vans were converted for traveling "back to the land" for homesteading and communal living experiments.

"Reaping": "...the Gilley family tale" as told in *John Gilley of Baker's Island* by Charles W. Eliot, president of Harvard University for forty years and prominent founder of the Northeast Harbor summer colony, was originally published in 1899 and again in 1904 under the title *John Gilley, Maine Farmer and Fisherman*. The story was reissued in 1985 by Acadia Press of Bar Harbor, Maine.

"Answering How Come You Always Rock The Baby": The poem read "through your mama's skin about coming out" is Brooks Haxton's poem to his unborn son, "Coming Out," *Traveling Company*, Knopf, 1989. Words and music to "Too-ra-loo-ra-loo-ral, That's an Irish Lullaby," are by James R. Shannon for Shameen Dhu musical theatre, 1914. Revived in 1944 by Bing Crosby and Barry Fitzgerald in *Going My Way*, musical film. "I Had a Little Doggy" is a song passed down in my mother's family that we've not been able to find published or performed since her mother heard a gramophone rendition in the 1920s. A barely recognizable version appears as a poem, no author given, in *The Home Book of Verse*, Henry Holt and Company, 1912. For our folk arrangement, see "Mamie's Lullaby."

"Quest: For John Andrews Called Old Buck": I am indebted to Sherman Alexie whose poetry, published by Hanging Loose press among others, is a just sentence. These words from "Scalp Dance of Spokane Indians," fired my "Quest...", "Always trying to steal a little bit of soul, you know? Whether it/be poetry or oils on canvas. They call themselves artists but they/are really archaeologists." As did this May 13, 1994 *Bangor Daily News* account: "Micmac Indians...have begun a 280-mile spiritual walk to seek direction from departed ancestors....The number of silent walkers is expected to reach about 1,000, according to Clarence Patles from Eel

Brunswick,...representatives of bands from Restigouce, Big Cove, Indian Island, Red Bank, Burnt Church, the Aroostook Band of Micmacs and their sister tribe, the Maliseets of Tobique. Patles invited people of other races and faiths to walk with them."

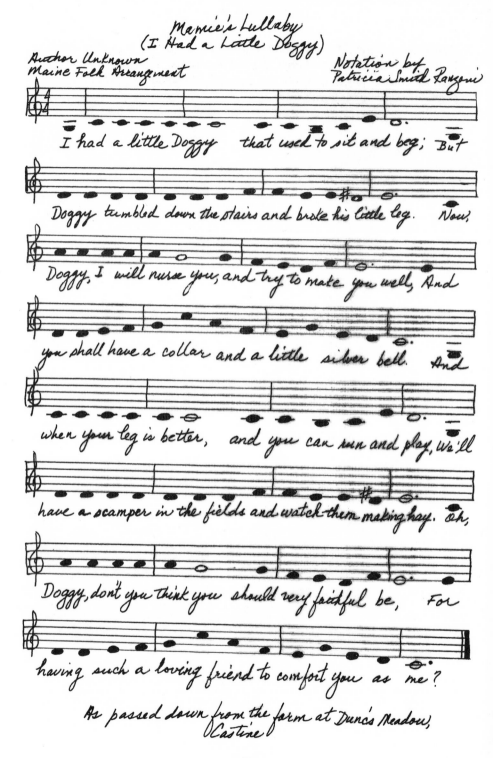

Mamie's Lullaby
(I Had a Little Doggy)

Author Unknown
Maine Folk Arrangement

Notation by
Patricia Smith Ranzoni

I had a little Doggy that used to sit and beg; But

Doggy tumbled down the stairs and broke his little leg. Now,

Doggy, I will nurse you, and try to make you well, And

you shall have a collar and a little silver bell. And

when your leg is better, and you can run and play, We'll

have a scamper in the fields and watch them making hay. Oh,

Doggy, don't you think you should very faithful be, For

having such a loving friend to comfort you as me?

As passed down from the farm at Dunc's Meadow,
Castine

90